WINNING
TOURNAMENT
KARATE

WINNING
TOURNAMENT
KARATE

BY
CHUCK NORRIS

WARNING

This book is presented only as a means of preserving a unique aspect of the heritage of the martial arts. Neither Ohara Publications nor the author makes any representation, warranty or guarantee that the techniques described or illustrated in this book will be safe or effective in any self-defense situation or otherwise. You may be injured if you apply or train in the techniques of self-defense illustrated in this book, and neither Ohara Publications nor the author is responsible for any such injury that may result. It is essential that you consult a physician regarding whether or not to attempt any technique described in this book. Specific self-defense responses illustrated in this book may not be justified in any particular situation in view of all of the circumstances or under the applicable federal, state or local law. Neither Ohara Publications nor the author makes any representation or warranty regarding the legality or appropriateness of any technique mentioned in this book.

OHARA ▯ PUBLICATIONS, INCORPORATED

SANTA CLARITA, CALIFORNIA

DEDICATION

To my wife Dianne, who has always stood by me—win or lose.

ACKNOWLEDGEMENT

I would like to express my appreciation to the many black belts who have trained with me and helped develop a system many feel is second to none.

My special thanks to Pat Johnson, Bob Wall and my brother Aaron.

ABOUT
THE
AUTHOR

When Chuck Norris began studying Tang Soo Do in Korea 15 years ago, it probably didn't occur to him that it would become a lifetime career. Since that time, his karate activities have taken him into teaching, tournament competition, television, cinema and he has become one of the most recognized names in the martial arts business.

His first major tournament win, the 1965 Winter Nationals in San Jose, California, started him off on a series of championship wins that have firmly seated his name on a list of top tournament competitors of our time. Among his victories are the titles of the International Grand Championships in Long Beach and the All-American New York Grand Championships, both for two consecutive years (1967 and 1968). He also won the National Tournament of Champions in Washington, D.C., earned the Triple Crown title for his high number of major tournament wins and became BLACK BELT MAGAZINE's Fighter of the Year for 1969. His major accomplishment was winning the Professional World Middleweight title in 1968 at Madison Square Garden.

After proving himself a fighter, Norris then established himself as a teacher by training a team of competitors who went undefeated for 29 tournaments, and he is now serving as commissioner of the new National Karate League.

Norris sees himself as a teacher now, but has found his career branching into other areas as well. He made his film debut with Dean Martin in "The Wrecking Crew" in 1968, and since then he has starred in "Return of the Dragon" (with Bruce Lee) and "Yellow Faced Tiger." He has made TV appearances on "The Flip Wilson Show," "The Johnny Carson Show," "The Mike Douglas Show," "The Merv Griffin Show" and "To Tell the Truth."

Norris and his wife, Dianne, have two sons, Mike (age 12) and Eric (age 9), and the entire family is proficient in the art. Both of his boys, for instance, have won titles in their own divisions.

"If you are physically, mentally and emotionally prepared, you'll win," says Norris. "This is the philosophy that makes my students good students—this is the philosophy that makes my fighters great fighters—and this is the philosophy I live by."

PREFACE

by

John Robertson

A man once stated in print that a good street fighter could defeat any karate tournament champion. As it is with most generalizations, this comment simply doesn't hold water. Of course we all know of karate tournament fighters, from white belt all the way up to black belt, who have been beaten by very ordinary street fighters. However, to say that ALL tournament champions can be defeated by a "Lochinvar" of the streets is a might wild. The rules which prevail in karate tournaments are geared toward competitiveness, so that one contestant doesn't slaughter the other outright. But because of these competitive rules, it often happens that a contestant will beat a superior fighter with an impotent flyswat, on which he somehow scored a point. Once ahead in points, he has merely to outrun his opponent for the remaining minutes.

It is competitors of this ilk who give tournament karate a bad name, but they are well worth stomaching for the greater number of sports-loving and truly competitive young people in the sport.

For this reason and for their sake, I have been spurred to collaborate in the production of this text, the point of which is to show the folly of modern American karate. We have been attempting to make sport karate adhere to the ancient dogmas in the midst of a totally modern and foreign environment—and we should not!

Sport karate and the ancient art of karate are from the same litter, but they are different cats. In other words, while a tournament champion should be expected to be a master of the art's form (*kata*), he should also be expected to be a master of its power, and thereby, of men.

It is therefore the purpose of this text to show you the quickest and most effective way to a tournament crown. I do not promise that it will be the same as that taught in some karate schools, but what IS learned in the legitimate schools will prepare you for this program if you are willing to change and win.

I have studied under Chuck Norris since 1964 and have watched him grow into the World Champion and initiator of a truly Americanized karate. It is not difficult for a person who is extraordinary to become a champion in certain areas, with a good bit of work and concentration. But when that person can reproduce himself in ordinary young people, and see champions come forth, then you may say that he has arrived at a zenith in his field.

Observing the Norris phenomenon over the years, as a psychologist and a practitioner of karate, I have been forcefully struck by a number of the qualities which set him apart.

ECLECTIC

After thoroughly learning the Korean art of *tang soo do*, Chuck Norris wasn't afraid to leave the pack and innovate this style of karate so that it would become effective for him under tournament free-fighting conditions. He is truly multi-styled in his approach to karate and his hands, which first reflected Japanese styles, have since become much more American in speed and spontaneity.

AMERICANIZED

Chuck Norris has both respect and great pride in his parent tang soo do system, but he would be doing the art a disservice in refusing to fit it into our own unique national frame. He has placed his innovative emphasis on aggressiveness and achieved a more sensible balance between its offensive and defensive moves.

QUADRIVESTIGIAL

Most styles of karate implement either a predominance of hand techniques or foot techniques in their classical interpretations. Chuck was quick to see the tremendous advantage of achieving a balance between the use of hands and feet as weapons. The novel approach removed the predictability which handcuffed fighters who relied on one or the other too heavily and in the long run, increased his stockpile of weapons from two to four—a quadrivestigial fighter.

TRANSFER

I have always been intrigued by the way Chuck Norris could train average students to achieve great goals in all forms of tournament karate. The wins started rolling in very quickly and today, our win-loss ratio in major tournaments is unequalled by any other karate school in the U.S. Our black belt teams have over eighty wins without a loss in world black belt competition at this writing.

* * * * * * *

Because of the above-mentioned qualities, we decided to collaborate on a text which would bring our discoveries and formulae to the average karate student, in hope of giving him a winner's edge. We know they are working principles because they have been repeated over and again by winning students across the nation.

A word of caution is in order, however. There is nothing magic about this text. You can't sleep with it under your pillow or grind it up and eat it with milk and sugar and expect to become proficient in the material it offers. Equally useless would be a simple reading of the pages. This book was written to be of value only as an action directive. You must enact these pages on the mat, until the speed blitzes and sparring drills become reflexive.

SPIRIT

Those who have had the pleasure of knowing Chuck Norris will not be hard-pressed to admit that he has an indomitable spirit. He is friendly and easy-going, but fiercely competitive at the same time. He has never gone out on the mat to be a good loser.

BELIEF IN SELF

Without succumbing to what is commonly called an "ego-trip," Chuck Norris rates extremely high in self-confidence. Once his winning formula was perfected, he could accept only one verdict—"winner." There is that calm assurance within the man that he has done all of his homework, and thus deserves the best of grades. He once remarked that he had never lost a match, and after seeing my look of disbelief (because he has lost matches and would be the first to admit it), he laughingly pointed out his meaning.

"A man only loses a match," he said, "when he broods over his loss. But if you learn from that loss, it becomes a major victory and puts you one more rung up the ladder of achievement. I don't call that losing."

MENTAL IMAGES

I have sat with Chuck when he was about to fight and watched him become preoccupied with an inner conflict. He was watching mental images of himself fighting his upcoming opponent. In this way, Chuck had prepared himself by mentally fighting out all of the possible counters and attacks he was to use against that opponent in a few short minutes—a distinct advantage. Chuck has told me many times that he gained points on his opponent with the exact moves that had beaten the opponent in his mind minutes earlier!

Scientific data has indicated that the mind can use these mental drills as a good replacement when actual experience is not possible. With the right degree of concentration, this mental sparring is often all that is necessary to prepare yourself immediately before a tournament fight.

HOW TO STUDY THE TEXT

A) Correct Learning Sequence—Before studying this book with any degree of concentration, read it in its entirety. This will give you an overview of all of the material presented as well as an idea where you are going and why you are going there, once you finally do begin to study. Once this is achieved, it is important that you apply yourself to learning this material *in the chronological order that is presented*. This will prevent you from developing any bad form and reinforcing it through practice, and will also guard against any gaps in your learning.

There are many aspects of karate but all of them fall into at least one of three fundamentals: *technique, power* and *speed*.

B) Technique—We feel it is absolutely necessary that a student learn EXACTLY how a technique is performed, and we insist that he must not go on to developing power or speed until he can reproduce the moves perfectly. Never allow yourself to make an incorrect move without immediately correcting it on a second try. One of the bigger problems in teaching karate is due to the desire of everyone to become a black belt. The beginner is looking so hard at the *dan*-rank that he does not have time to learn mere white belt techniques.

Since true power is derived not from muscle, but from technique, it should be obvious that this phase cannot be entered until your form in a particular technique is perfect. The same can be said of speed. Every school has its "flailers" who slap weak, ineffectual punches in the air. They are perfect examples of what happens when you do not first perfect your technique or fail to practice things in the order they are offered.

In practicing your technique, begin performing in ultra slow motion and repeat it until you have reproduced the move perfectly. This very important point will be stressed again with more detail in the "Graduated Speed Drills" section.

C) Reading—As previously mentioned, you should allow yourself to "pre-read" the contents of this book so you may get a general outlook as to its contents. Following this, you should re-read the book at a slower pace and finally, when this is completed, begin your intensive study. Make use of these reading techniques as follows:

Pre-read
Re-read

1. Try to remember the broad outline of each chapter.
2. Make note of all the headings, emphasized words and key points including the pictures.
3. Relate the pictures to these points.
4. Underline all key points in pencil and don't be hesitant to write your own comments in the margins.

Intensive Study: At this point, you should be "saturation learning." Be sure that you understand each point before going on to the next—don't be afraid at this point to get up and try the techniques in ultra slow motion.

D) Practice of the Drills—The drill sessions are presented in two parts, mental drills and physical drills. It is easy for a student to neglect the mental drills, but be assured that to do so would be a mistake. If you can't do it in your mind, you certainly won't be able to do it with your body. *Practice the following "Graduated Speed Drills" first mentally and then physically.*

GRADUATED SPEED DRILLS

Each technique in this text should be practiced along the lines of a "graduated speed" which will allow you to learn perfect form and retain it as you gain power and speed slowly but surely. You should NOT go from one speed to the next unless the form of each technique remains perfect at that speed.

A) **Slow Motion**—Each and every technique should first be practiced in a dream-like slow motion. Read the captions, apply them to the pictures and go through the technique as slowly as you possibly can, making sure that you are doing it correctly as it appears. When you can consistently perform a technique perfectly, you may go on to the next speed.

B) **Half Speed**—The transition to this speed in terms of rhythm, focus, balance and all other phases of karate technique is not an easy one. It is still a rather slow motion, but should be much smoother without sacrificing a single bit of perfection in your technique. Be sure you do not push your speed too high at this point, as it should still be considered a rather slow motion. Also, flex your muscles tightly at the end of each motion so you will have some semblance of power.

C) **Full Speed**—After you are satisfied that you have mastered a perfect form at half speed, practice the very same form at the fullest speed of which you are capable. At this point, the tendency is to get sloppy, so pay particular attention to your form, making sure that it is not sacrificed at this speed. Do not become discouraged if your form seems to leave you at this speed, for it will certainly come back after judicial practice and concentration. Be patient and practice. Do not end a workout without having performed the technique *ten* consecutive times without a mistake.

D) **Red Line**—The purpose of "Red Line" is twofold. First, it will give you a good workout and enhance your stamina. Secondly, it will push your full speed ability to new and greater heights. "Red Line" calls for you to achieve a speed faster than you've ever before attained. It is an open-ended drill with the emphasis on your constant attainment of more and more speed. As always, it is very important that you maintain excellence in your form, although some technique may be sacrificed to speed. Utilize the drill correctly and you will find yourself performing beyond your former capabilities. Perform it incorrectly and it will destroy your technique.

E) **Mixing It Up**—After you have begun to improve your speed through the "Red Line" drill, we have found that mixing speeds often provides a good drill for control in your rhythm, your balance and your form. Begin the longer techniques in slow motion and go from one speed to another, quarter speed, half speed, full speed and "Red Line" in the process of performing that same technique. Continually strive for perfect balance, rhythm and form in doing all of these drills, and watch your ability rise.

THE "GETTING STARTED" COUNTDOWN

5. Read over the materials to be sure you are familiar with them.
4. Find a place where you will not be disturbed.
3. Get situated comfortably.
2. Get mentally set for concentration and learning.
1. Assume the "ready to move" stance (basic fighting stance or short forward stance).
0. Practice, correct, practice, master!

by John Robertson

CONTENTS

INTRODUCTION

This volume is structured to give you the basic foundation on which a championship style can be built. The teaching method herein acknowledges your individuality and is geared toward teaching you how you may adapt this foundation to your own unique self.

The text has been divided into sections, first showing you how to study the text, and then concentrating on the mechanics such as conditioning, attacks and technical excellence. It is designed to be studied as a whole and is not going to benefit you if you take a "cafeteria" approach, picking and choosing one thing or another. It is much like a chain, each link depending upon the strength of the link which precedes it.

ATTACKS

The moves in this section will give you a good idea of how to press an opening attack, as well as how to deal with an opponent who specializes in doing the unexpected. The key here is practice, a constant repetition that will improve your timing and most important of all, render your attacks reflexive. If practiced properly, you will not need to think during a match, but simply act and react.

One of the most important moments in every tournament match is the *initial move*. It can be either a feint (a maneuver to fake the opponent into thinking that you are about to attack) or an actual attack. Using the feint will generally tell you a great deal about your opponent, whether he is a retreater, a counterman or a "sitter." The feint can also be used to set up your opponent for an attack, the timing of which is equally as important as the feint. If these gambits are correctly used, you will find a new edge to your attack, and a much higher point average in your matches.

THE INITIAL MOVE

One of the most difficult things about karate free-sparring is getting inside your opponent's defenses with your attacks. For this reason, you should make use of your initial move to bring about a reaction from your opponent, and then counter-react to it. Your opponent's reaction will usually dictate your own mode of attack. Other factors are involved, however. One is your *personality aggression level.*

A passive personality will usually hesitate to attack, and should pay special attention to the "Aggression Builder" section which appears in a later volume. The very aggressive personality has a different problem. Overly aggressive persons are often disqualified for unnecessary roughness or lack of control. People with this problem will find solutions in the "Control" section of the next volume.

Still another factor of judgement in your initial move is the personality of your opponent. Is he a retreater or a counterattacker? Upon finding out what type of fighter he is, you should make adjustments in your own attack. For instance, if you charge an opponent with a good set of combinations, you will be blown out of the ring if you are not careful. If you employ a like attack on a retreater, he will be halfway into the grandstands by the time your kick is in mid-air. The main point is to know what your opponent is going to do when you attack—BEFORE YOU ATTACK!

INITIAL MOVE No. 1

(1) Begin by facing your opponent in a fighting stance.
(2) Lean your weight on your front leg and feint a left lunge punch at his head.
Your opponent's reaction will give you good insight into his fighting style. This first move is strictly a feint and not a set-up. Remember that the feint should be convincing and therefore should be made up of the same moves you would use when actually employing an attack.

INITIAL MOVE No. 2

(1) Begin by facing your opponent in a left forward fighting stance. (2) Lean your weight on your front leg and feint a left lunge punch at his head. (3) Allow a split second of time for your opponent to react to the feint. (4) Lunge forward off your rear leg and execute a right reverse punch to his ribs.

This gambit makes use of your opponent's high defense against your feint and is also too quick for him to reverse directions and run.

CLOSING THE GAP

The single most important phase of making the initial move is closing the gap which separates you and your opponent. In fact, it is a consummate art form which often separates the good fighter from the mediocre one. If your opponent is the type of fighter who stands his ground and does not retreat with your every movement, certain closing moves will help you in gaining the points you want at the start of the match. If your opponent is, in fact, a retreater, you may do one of two things. You may have an attacking opener which works from a distance, or you may sit him out and have a strong counter set for him when he charges. Be careful not to be lulled into confidence by a man who prefers setting a large distance between the two of you, for a good fighter can make a devastating attack from a distance.

The ideal situation would be to train yourself for an expertise in distance attacks, one move attacks and counterattacks.

One of the most effective ways that you can conceal your intent to close the gap between you and your opponent, is to be in constant motion. The man who takes a rigid "Rock of Gibraltar" stance will not be able to deceive anyone when he finally decides to launch forward. As Pat Johnson once noted, attacks from such a stationary posture have all the surprise of a wall that suddenly moves. In order to catch your opponent off-guard with your attacks, *you must be in constant motion!* You must be loose, with your weight on the balls of your feet—ready to move in any direction to block, strike or counterattack. This is not to say that you should be running all over the ring, but confine your constant motion to a boxer's bounce, side-stepping, moving back and forward and generally keeping your opponent constantly off-guard.

When you finally do close the gap, never do so without employing or planning to employ an attacking maneuver.

CLASSICAL CLOSING TECHNIQUE

(1) Begin by assuming a left forward fighting stance with your fists held at medium height. (2) Lean most of your weight on your forward leg, while maintaining your hands in their original positions. (3 & 4) Step quickly ahead with your rear leg so that you achieve a right forward fighting stance and simultaneously execute a right lunge punch.

This classical stepping punch, though good for focus and power, will leave you open and at your opponent's mercy during a tournament match. Unless you can fill in the gaps with additional striking techniques, you will be defeating your own purpose with an attack of this type.

APPLICATION (WRONG)

(1) Face your opponent in a right forward fighting stance. (2 & 3) It is easy to see the folly of the classical stepping punch which leaves you open to a left reverse punch to your head before you have even finished your step-through.

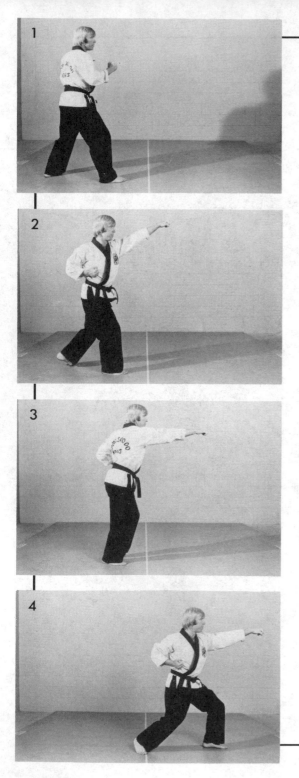

PRACTICAL CLOSING TECHNIQUE

(1) Begin in a right forward fighting stance with your fists held at medium height. (2) Begin your step by placing most of your weight on your forward leg and execute a left reverse punch. (3) Move your rear leg ahead and execute a right punch as it becomes even with your other leg. (4) Step your rear leg completely through so that you achieve a left forward fighting stance and simultaneously execute a left lunge punch.

The aggressiveness of this closing technique effectively fills in the gaps of your movement, keeping your opponent on the defensive and allowing you to get the point. It is important at this point to be sure and vary the targets of your punches. Don't throw them all at the head.

THE LUNGE

The lunge is a relatively short-range technique, usually between 8 and 12 inches in length along the floor. For this reason, it is one of the fastest ways in which you can close the gap, and also one of the most powerful. The lunge can be initiated from a variety of stances successfully. The straddle stance and the back stance are just a couple of examples. But it is most effectively employed from the fighting stance, which closely resembles the classical karate forward stance, though not quite as deep or stationary.

Once you have committed your mind to launching a lunge attack, be sure you do not telegraph your intentions by bobbing or leaning. The lunge should be a single, smooth motion without the jerking and leaning forward which would apprise your opponent of your intentions.

PERFORMING THE LUNGE

(1) Begin by assuming a left forward fighting stance. (2) Being careful to keep your upper torso erect and motionless, lift your front foot slightly off the floor while you thrust your body forward with your rear foot. (3) Allow yourself to travel about 12 inches forward, being sure to drag your rear foot across the floor for balance and (4) come to rest in the fighting position, ready to execute your attack. This technique should be practiced to a point where you can begin executing your attack in the middle of your lunge.

LUNGE
APPLICATION No. 1
(Versus a Standing Opponent)

(1) When you have ascertained that your opponent is NOT a counterattacker through feints, you may decide to commit yourself to a lunge attack from the fighting stance. (2) Begin the lunge while you simultaneously begin your right reverse punch attack. (3 & 4) As you have closed the gap, execute the right reverse punch attack and be sure to follow through by strengthening your stance. You are now in a position to employ follow-up attacking combinations, keeping your opponent on the defensive by executing a battery of fist attacks.

LUNGE APPLICATION No. 2
(Versus a Countering Opponent)

(1) From the fighting stance, execute a feint on your opponent to force a commitment on his part. (2) As your opponent takes the feint and attempts a right reverse punch, initiate your forward lunge while you simultaneously execute a right reverse punch. (3) In order to keep your opponent on the defensive, immediately execute a right front kick to his midsection. (4) Drop your kicking foot straight down to the floor and execute a left reverse punch to the midsection as you retract your right fist to your hip for power. (5) From your left reverse punch posture, grab your opponent's right arm with your left hand and begin to sweep his forward leg with your rear foot. (6) Sweep your opponent's forward leg inward as you pull outward with your grasping hand, causing him to lose balance. (7 & 8) As your opponent hits the floor, maintain your grasp of his shoulder and execute a right reverse punch to his face.

LUNGE APPLICATION No. 3
(Versus a Charging Opponent)

(1) Begin by facing your opponent in the fighting position. (2) As your opponent initiates a charging attack, (a front kick in this case), begin executing your forward lunge. (3&4) As you lunge forward inside his kicking attack, simultaneously execute a left lunge punch to his face. (5) Grasp your opponent's chest with your right hand while you neutralize his right arm with your left. (6) Turn 180 degrees counterclockwise on your forward leg and (7) execute a shoulder throw with your left hand grasping his forearm and your right hand grasping his tricep area. (8) As your opponent hits the floor, maintain your left hand grip while you execute a right back knuckle strike to the face.

LUNGE APPLICATION No. 4
(Versus a Retreating Opponent)

(1) Begin by facing your opponent in the fighting stance. (2) After having judged that your opponent will definitely retreat if attacked, begin stepping your rear leg forward and grasp his sleeve with your forward hand. (3) As your opponent turns to retreat, check the back of his forward knee with your right foot. (4) Being sure to maintain your grasp, drop your right foot to the floor and execute a right lunge punch to the head. (5) Still maintaining your grasp, pivot clockwise on your right foot and execute a left roundhouse kick to the groin. (6) Return your kicking leg to the floor while swiveling your hips counterclockwise, and execute a right reverse punch to your opponent's head. (7) Bring your punching hand down to grasp your opponent's near shoulder, and pull outward while executing an inward right foot sweep on his forward leg. (8) As your opponent hits the floor, execute a left reverse punch to his chest.

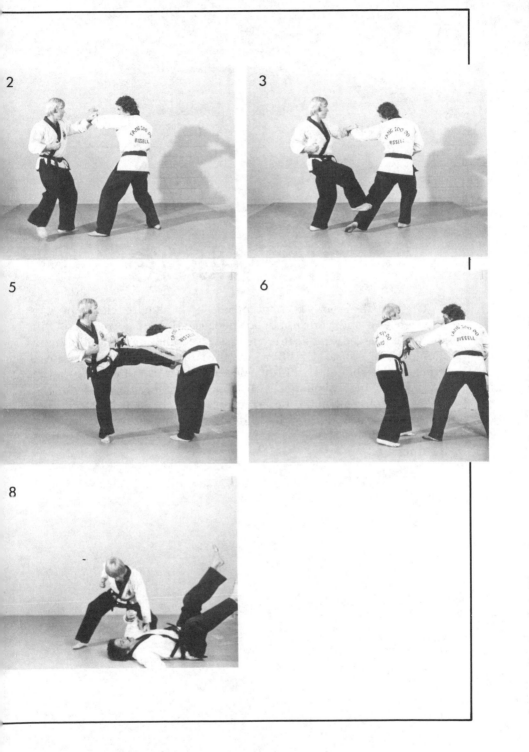

THE SHUFFLE

The shuffle is an excellent means by which to close the gap between you and your opponent because, if done correctly, it will give you the advantage of surprise. Keeping in mind that you should be in constant motion, the initial part of the shuffle move, which is the slide-up, will not telegraph your intention to press an attack. The best opener in your attacking combination from the shuffle, would usually be a reverse punch, which should be smoothly begun during the slide-up and make contact as you complete the step. The step and punch should always land together.

PERFORMING
THE SHUFFLE

(1) Begin by standing erect in the fighting stance. (2) Perform a hand feint as you slide your rear leg into your forward leg. (3) Step ahead with your forward leg approximately 12 to 18 inches.

This method of closing the gap should be used against an opponent whose distance from you is not more than two or three feet. As you practice this movement, concentrate on keeping your upper torso erect so that your head does not bob during the slide-up. You should be able to do it without any noticeable change in body height.

SHUFFLE
WITH COMBINATION

(1) Begin by standing erect in the fighting stance. (2) Execute a high feint with your forward fist as you begin the step-up by placing most of your weight on your forward leg. (3) Bring your rear foot into your forward foot. (4) Step forward 12 to 18 inches with your stationary leg while you simultaneously execute a right reverse punch to the midsection.

SHUFFLE
APPLICATION No. 1
(Versus a Standing Opponent)

(1) Begin by facing your opponent in the fighting stance. (2 & 3) Feint a left high punch in order to force your opponent to commit himself while you simultaneously step your rear leg into your forward leg. (4) Step ahead with your forward leg while you simultaneously execute a right reverse punch to the midsection.

SHUFFLE
APPLICATION No. 2
(Versus a Countering Opponent)

(1) Begin by facing your opponent in the fighting stance. (2 & 3) Feint a left punch at your opponent's head, forcing him to initiate a counter, while you simultaneously step your rear foot into your forward foot.

(4) Step ahead with your forward foot while you simultaneously execute a right reverse punch to your opponent's ribs. (This application bears a marked likeness to that used against a standing opponent, except your punch will be thrown under the opponent's countering arm instead of inside it.) (5) Following your reverse punch, grab your opponent's shoulder with your right hand and execute a right foot sweep to his forward leg. (6) Should the foot sweep fail to cause your opponent to lose his balance, be prepared to drop your right foot to the floor and execute a left roundhouse instep kick to his chin.

SHUFFLE
APPLICATION No. 3
(Versus a Retreating Opponent)

(1) Begin by facing your opponent in the fighting stance. (2 & 3) Feint a left punch at your opponent's head while you simultaneously step your rear foot into your forward foot. (4) Without allowing your opponent enough time to begin his retreat, quickly step your forward foot ahead and simultaneously execute a right reverse punch to the midsection.

THE STEP-THROUGH

As an attacking opener, the step-through technique provides great potential for power as well as a means by which to cover a little over two feet of distance between yourself and your opponent. This type of attack maneuver is very difficult to counter or escape without being pointed because it is a natural maneuver that allows you to keep maximum balance. When used with the "fill-in-the-gap" policy of throwing a battery of punches while taking the step, it can have a bewildering effect on your opponent.

PERFORMING THE STEP-THROUGH

(1) Begin in the fighting stance with your fists held at medium height. (2) Lean most of your weight on your forward leg while you execute a high right reverse punch. (3) Begin to slide your rear foot forward while you execute a high left punch. (4) Complete the step-through of your rear leg so that it is about a shoulder's width in front of your other foot and execute a right punch.

It is important to throw multiple punches while you perform the step-through attack in order to keep your opponent at bay. Also, it is important that you do not take too long a step (24 inches would be sufficient) as it would serve to dissipate the power of the attack.

STEP-THROUGH
APPLICATION No. 1
(Versus a Standing Opponent)

(1) Begin by facing your opponent in the fighting stance. (2) Step forward with your rear foot while you execute a right high punch at the head of your opponent. (3 & 4) Complete the step-through of your rear foot and as your opponent reacts to your high punch, execute a left medium punch to his midsection.

STEP-THROUGH
APPLICATION No. 2
(Versus a Countering Opponent)

(1) Begin by facing your opponent in the fighting stance. (2) Force your opponent to commit himself to a counter by executing a left high punch as you place your weight on your forward leg. (3 & 4) Begin moving your rear foot forward

while you continue to keep your opponent at bay with a right high punch. (5) Complete the step-through of your rear foot while you simultaneously execute a left punch to his unprotected midsection.

STEP-THROUGH APPLICATION No. 3
(Versus a Retreating Opponent)

(1) Begin by facing your opponent in the fighting stance. (2) Quickly execute a right high punch at your opponent's face while you place your weight on your forward leg. (3) Step through with your rear foot while you bring your right hand down slightly and grasp the lapel of your opponent's gi. (4) Maintaining your grasp so your opponent cannot retreat, execute a left reverse punch to his midsection.

THE SLIDE-UP LUNGE

The slide-up lunge maneuver is effective as an attacking opener when you and your opponent are separated by a gap of up to five feet. If practiced properly, it will allow you to close a wide gap without having telegraphed your intentions to your opponent. The slide-up portion of the move in particular can go wholly unnoticed by your opponent, leaving him unprepared for the lunge that is to follow.

PERFORMING
THE SLIDE-UP LUNGE

(1) Begin by assuming a fighting stance with your fists held at medium height. (2) Slide your rear foot quickly into your front foot without bobbing your head or upper torso. (3-5) Execute a forward lunge off the foot which slid forward, being sure to drag that foot along the floor be-

hind you during the lunge.
In order to see how this maneuver may be used against the varied opponents (the standing opponent, the countering opponent and the retreating opponent), refer to the applications offered previously in the lunge section of this book.

THE STEP-THROUGH LUNGE

The step-through lunge is also useful in closing a large gap between yourself and your opponent. This technique is effective anywhere between 18 inches and five feet, and is difficult to counter. Opponents are often lulled into believing that it will cover much less distance than it actually does, since the opening motion appears to be a single step.

PERFORMING THE STEP-THROUGH LUNGE

(1) Begin by assuming the fighting stance with your fists held at medium height. (2) Lean your weight on your forward leg and begin stepping forward with your rear foot. (3-5) Continue stepping your leg forward and, rather than simply stepping through, lunge ahead on your stationary foot for the desired distance, being sure to drag that foot along the floor behind you for balance.

In order to see how this maneuver may be used against the varied opponents, refer to the applications offered in the lunge section of this book.

JUMPING KICKS

When an opponent is separated from you by a very great distance, you may also opt to make use of a jumping kick. There are many types of jumping kicks, most of which will be treated later in the conditioning portion of this text. These techniques should be used sparingly, however, as they will leave you vulnerable to counters. Jumping kicks should never be used unless you can consistently strike a three inch target circle. In other words, unless you are reasonably sure you can score a point with your accuracy, you should never employ a jumping kick. There are other guidelines to keep in mind before committing yourself to such a tactic. They are:

1. Make extensive use of initial moves, feints and the like, so that you may evaluate your opponent thoroughly.

2. Never employ a jumping kick without preceding it with a fake kick.

3. Always jump up and into your opponent in such a way and with such force that he will be struck if he does not move. Jump so that your landing point will be well past the point where your opponent is standing.

4. Always continue the attack as you land. Unleash a battery of punches and possibly even kicks the moment you touch the ground.

5. Use the jumping kick as part of a run-down technique. Remember that you are closing the gap and that the jumping kicks can be used effectively as a means to catch a retreating opponent, particularly when he is back pedaling.

6. Use the jumping kicks as infrequently as possible, so your opponent will not be able to predict or anticipate this vulnerable method of attack.

PERFORMING THE JUMPING SIDE KICK

(1) Begin by assuming the fighting stance and raise your arms in preparation for a jump. (2) Jump up and into your target with both feet leaving the floor. (3) Execute a side kick with your forward foot while angling your rear foot toward the floor.

Additional jumping kicks are offered in the "Conditioning" section.

ATTACKING TECHNIQUES

Attacking techniques are of great value in chasing down a "running" opponent and scoring on him. The emphasis must be placed on supreme technical excellence and total aggressiveness of attack. The moves offered on the following pages are geared toward giving you the ability and sophistication to attack with finesse and power. They should be approached from three directions:

1. Learn the technique offered on the following pages. Be sure you are able to perform it perfectly within a matter of seconds.

2. Make up a series of your own attacking techniques, using those strikes and kicks which you feel are best suited to your style of attack.

3. Perform impromptu attacking techniques across the mat. Make them spontaneous and without forethought. In other words, they should become automatic to you.

SAMPLE
ATTACKING TECHNIQUE

(1) Begin by assuming a left forward stance with your fists at medium height. (2 & 3) Lunge forward off your rear foot and execute a high left lunge punch as you come to rest in another left forward fighting stance.

(4) Maintaining your stance, execute a left down block. (5-7) Pivot your body around clockwise on your forward foot, using your momentum in the execution of a right bottom fist strike, which should make contact at the close of your 180-degree clockwise turn. (8-10) Pivot your body 180 degrees counterclockwise on your left foot and execute a left outward knife hand block at the close of the turn. (11) Maintaining your left forward stance, turn your hips counterclockwise and execute a right reverse punch. (12) Immediately execute a right front kick from the same posture.

13

16

19

(13 & 14) Retract your kicking foot so that you are in a left fighting stance and simultaneously execute a left upward forearm block. (15) Execute a right reverse punch while retracting your left fist to your hip. (16 & 17) Maintaining your reverse punch posture, execute a right front kick. (18 & 19) As your kicking foot drops straight down to the floor, execute a right back knuckle strike from the right fighting stance. (20) Execute a left reverse punch while retracting your right fist to your hip.

CONDITIONING

Two of my seventeen-year-old students were recently taking the promotion test for green belt. When they came to the sparring portion of the exam, they were already winded from the forms and the hand-foot combinations they had just completed. The sparring had hardly begun before they were both exhausted, which resulted in their failing of the test. They were simply in terrible condition.

As conditioning is a major part of the boxing profession, so is it important to tournament karate. It should be placed on equal footing with forms, techniques and all other aspects of karate, for without it, the technical parts of karate cannot be achieved. If you cannot sustain your attacks because you are exhausted, you will lose the match as certainly as though you had poor technique.

The mere mention of the word, "conditioning" conjures

immediate visions of endless squats, push ups and so on. However, this does not have to be the case. There is a way to combine the reward of stamina that you gain through conditioning, with technical training as well. The following pages offer this new and more practical approach to conditioning.

Of course, you are still required to perform the warm-up exercises that will save you the trouble of nursing pulled muscles and the like. These standard warm-up exercises are not offered in this book, since you should already have a routine set for yourself before every practice session.

Be sure to approach this section with the same procedures you've used in the previous section, including the mental image drills, the repetitive practice, the speed variations, etc. Do not go from one exercise to the other without having fully mastered it.

KICKS ON THE HEAVY BAG

Kicking the heavy bag accomplishes several things. It teaches you to gauge your distance and realistically focus your kicks against a solid object. It also conditions your legs for lift and thrusting power. Giving the bag a push and kicking into its return improves your timing on a moving target. This simple addition will quickly show you what kind of stability your kicks have and will help you work to improve it.

FRONT KICK

(1) Begin in the fighting stance and push the heavy bag in the direction away from yourself. (2) As the bag begins to swing back toward you, bring your rear foot off the floor and begin to move it forward. (3) Execute a front kick, hitting the bag with the ball of your kicking foot as it becomes perpendicular to the floor. (4) Immediately follow the kick by retracting your kicking leg.

STEPPING
SIDE KICK

(1) Begin in a fighting stance and push the bag away from you. (2 & 3) As the bag begins to swing back toward you, bring your rear foot to your forward foot and cock your forward leg while

twisting your hips counter-clockwise. (4) Execute a side kick as the bag is approximately perpendicular to the floor. (5) Retract your kicking leg immediately following contact.

BACK KICK

(1) Push the bag away from you and step your rear foot into your forward foot. (2) As the bag begins to swing back toward you, turn your hips

counterclockwise and cock your forward foot. (3) Execute a back kick while looking over the shoulder nearest the target to assure accuracy.

TARGET KICK AND PUNCH

This multi-purposed drill holds many values for the student hoping to enter tournament karate successfully. Among them are:

ACCURACY: Doing this drill will consistently acquaint you with placing your kicks and strikes to the exact spot they were intended to hit.

TIMING: This drill will also sharpen your timing, since you will be gauging the contact points on more than one target that has been dropped.

REFLEXES: More than anything else, this drill will work on your reflex actions, since you are required to strike targets that are free-falling toward the floor.

FOLLOW-THROUGH: There will be no need to pull your punches or kicks just short of contact since you are not throwing your blows at another person. Instead, you may strike beyond the surface of the target.

SPEED: In order to consistently hit both falling targets, you will have to develop great speed in striking and kicking.

FOCUS: This drill will increase the power in your punching and kicking techniques if you can concentrate on maintaining good form during its entirety.

Target kicks are more difficult insofar as your legs will be slower than your arms. For this reason, your partner should hold the target higher, giving it a longer dropping distance and thereby compensating for the difference in speed. The reflex and timing value of these drills cannot be overstressed. Be sure that you do not sacrifice your technique in the process of gaining speed.

TARGET PUNCH DRILL No. 1

(1) Stand set in a fighting stance with your fists at your sides while a partner holds a cardboard target extended in front of you. (2) As your partner drops the target without warning you, execute a right reverse punch into the target.

This drill can be done with any variety of hand or fist strikes. The principal idea is to have the target dropped with as little telegraphing as possible. Only when the dropping of the target comes as a surprise can this drill have its maximum effect.

TARGET PUNCH DRILL No. 2

(1) Stand erect with your fists at your sides and your feet spread to shoulder width. Your partner should be holding two cardboard targets aloft and you should be facing the target which you intend to hit first.
(2 & 3) As your partner drops both targets in a one-two or bang-bang sequence, execute a straight right punch through the first one, and a right back knuckle strike through the second.
When you have become proficient in this drill, you should be able to strike both targets as they are dropped simultaneously. Practice this drill daily and do not leave it for the day unless you can execute both strikes perfectly on three consecutive tries.

71

TARGET KICK
DRILL No. 1

(1) Assume a fighting stance and face the single target which your partner is holding aloft. (2) As your partner releases the target, execute a front kick through the target. Use different kicks in this drill, keeping your emphasis on form as well as speed.

TARGET KICK DRILL No. 2

(1) Stand erect with your fists at your sides and your feet spread to shoulder width. Your partner should be holding two cardboard targets aloft and you should be facing the upper target which you intend to hit first. (2) As your partner releases the upper target, hit it with a roundhouse kick. (3) Immediately after releasing the first target, your partner should release the second, at which time you should retract your kicking leg slightly and hit it with another roundhouse kick.

Be sure to use this drill in perfecting all of your kicks (front, side, etc.) and when you become proficient, you should be able to kick both targets after they have been dropped at the same time.

TARGET KICK DRILL No. 3

(1) Have your partner hold a rectangular leather target bag aloft in one hand and stand ready about five feet away. (2) Bring your rear leg up quickly and (3) use its momentum in aiding you to jump up and forward toward the target. (4) While you are still airborne, quickly execute a roundhouse kick through

the target. (5) Retract
your kicking foot by bend-
ing your knee, and allow
your weight to land
squarely on your other
foot.
This drill will perfect your
jumping roundhouse kick,
a very effective attacking
opener that can be used
from great distances.

TARGET KICK DRILL No. 4

(1) Begin by standing approximately five feet from the target being held aloft in your partner's hand. (2) Slide your rear foot into your forward foot and begin raising your forward foot from the floor. (3) Execute a high roundhouse kick through the target with your forward foot. (4) Retract your kicking foot to a median position, from where you may either execute yet another roundhouse kick to the target, or drop it to the floor.

TARGET KICK DRILL No. 5

(1) Begin by standing approximately five feet from the target being held aloft in your partner's hand. (2) Slide your rear foot into your forward foot. (3) Raise your forward foot and execute a fake of a low roundhouse kick. (4) Bend your upper torso down toward the floor and from the fake kick position, execute a high roundhouse kick through the target.

In performing this particular drill, be sure that your fake kick is executed in such a way that it appears to be a real kick. There should only be a split second of time elapsing between the fake and the actual kick.

TARGET KICK
DRILL No. 6

(1) Begin by standing approximately five feet from the target being held aloft in your partner's hand and step through toward the target with your rear foot. (2) As the step-through is completed, immediately lift your foot off the floor and begin to move it forward. (3) Execute an outside crescent kick through the target, making contact with the outside blade of your foot. (4) Without breaking the outside circular follow-through of the kick, bring your kicking foot to the floor.

TARGET KICK
DRILL No. 7

(1) Begin by standing approximately five feet from the target being held aloft in your partner's hand. (2) Slide your rear foot into your forward foot. (3 & 4) Rotate your forward foot to the outside and execute a heel kick through the target. Be sure to follow through in a circular motion before bringing your kicking foot back to the floor.

TARGET KICK DRILL No. 8

(1) Begin by standing approximately five feet from the target being held aloft in your partner's hand. (2) Pivot your body counterclockwise on the ball of your forward foot as you move your rear foot forward.
(3 & 4) Continue to pivot

3

in the same direction while you lift your rear foot and execute a spinning heel kick through the target. (5) Follow through with the kick in the same direction so that you have gone beyond the target before allowing your foot to drop to the floor.

4

5

TARGET KICK
DRILL No. 9

(1) Begin by standing approximately five feet from the target being held aloft in your partner's hand. (2 & 3) Slide your rear leg into your forward leg. (4 & 5) Lift your forward foot off the floor and away from the target, and execute a heel kick through the target. (6) Follow all the way through with the kick so that your kicking foot touches the floor behind you on the side opposite the target. (7) Continue pivoting in the same direction on the ball of your forward foot. (8 & 9) Lift your rear foot off the floor once again and execute a spinning heel kick through the target.

This particular drill should be performed with speed and accuracy without sacrificing the form of the kicks.

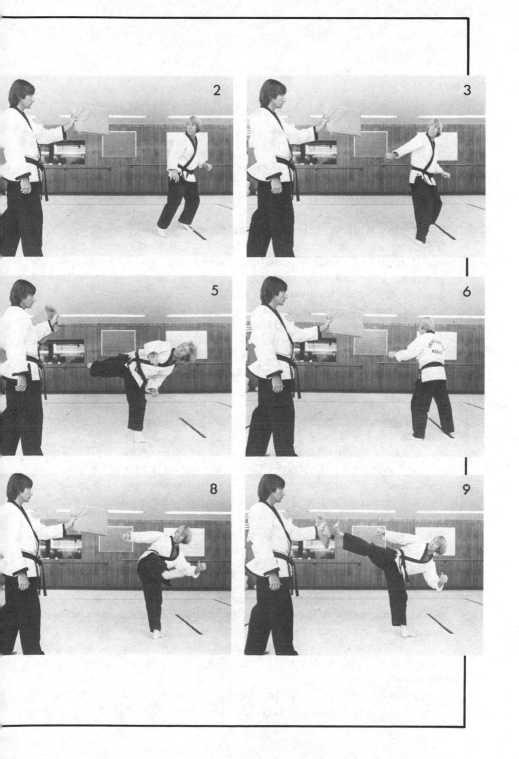

TECHNICAL EXCELLENCE

The "technique" facet of karate is just as important to the mastering of the martial art as is speed and conditioning. Tournament competitors in even the black belt division have been disqualified during their matches for the slovenly technique that has come to be known as "street fighting" among the referees. It is sad that such a thing is possible, and it is truly embarrassing to see someone who has achieved the highest belt level in karate flailing away in the ring like a petulant child.

One reason for this sad state of affairs seems to be poor instruction. The vogue these days seems to be throwing on a black belt and immediately opening a school. There is nothing wrong with charging a fair price for a commodity, but when that commodity is not offered, it becomes unethical and even criminal. Of course, some people will never be able to become good teachers, and this includes even the best of black belts. But the ability to transmit knowledge to others should be part of the requirements in making the dan-rank.

Another reason for poor technique would be the common malady known as "instant expertitis." It's hard to put a finger on the cause, but many people in this country are opposed to putting in the time it takes to accomplish expertise in anything, including karate. One of the first things a student wants to know upon enrollment is, "How long will it take to become a black belt?" It is the instructor's duty to see that these attitudes are changed and replaced by dedication and discipline in the mental, physical and emotional spheres.

The final reason is probably sheer laziness on the student's part. Good techniques in karate are difficult to learn and difficult to keep. It is little wonder, then, that most students will not exert the effort to learn. Unless the instructor has at least a spark of true desire with which to work, the lazy student will never master technique.

It is not the point of this text to go into the basics of karate technique, since that would divert us from your goal of winning

tournaments. It is, however, within this book's scope to offer you technique DRILLS which will enhance the basic techniques that you should already be familiar with. If the following drills are performed properly, they should increase your focus, power and speed. And to perform the following forms "properly," you should concentrate on the following: CORRECT MOVES—BALANCE—ENDURANCE—FOCUS—RHYTHM—TIMING—ACCURACY.

Another important point to remember in practicing the following forms is the need to perform them at varied speeds. Learning the forms at slow motion, half-speed, full-speed and red-line will help not only your technique, but your rhythm as well.

RHYTHM FORM (YI-DAN)

When learning the first drill, Rhythm Form I, concentrate on one segment at a time and add each new segment onto the previously learned ones. Vary your speed with the four phase approach. Remember, rhythm is never jerky or disconnected and yet no form should have the same rhythm throughout. Keep your balance throughout and don't increase your overall speed until you can do so without losing your technique.

(1) Begin by assuming the ready position with your fists held in front of your lower abdomen. (2 & 3) Cock your fists to the right and step your left foot to the side into a left forward stance as you simultaneously execute a high inside double block. (4 & 5) Turn your hips counterclockwise and execute a right uppercut punch while grasping downward into your right shoulder with your left fist. (6) Draw your left foot in toward your right and execute a fake of a right reverse punch. (7) Move your left foot forward into a horse stance and execute a left side punch. (8 & 9) Turn your upper torso clockwise and achieve a right back stance as you execute a high double block. (10 & 11) Grasp downward toward your left shoulder with your right fist while you execute a left uppercut punch.

(12) Draw your right foot in toward your left and execute a fake of a left reverse punch. (13) Step your right foot ahead into a horse stance and simultaneously execute a right side punch. (14) Step your left foot into your right and turn your upper torso 90 degrees clockwise. (15 & 16) Simultaneously execute a right bottom fist strike and a right side kick. (17) Drop your kicking foot to the floor, turn your head to the opposite side and achieve a right back stance while you execute a high left knife hand strike. (18) Step your right foot ahead, past your left, so that you achieve a right back stance, and execute a high right knife hand strike. (19) Step your left foot past your right so that you achieve a left back stance and execute a high

left knife hand strike. (20 & 21) Step your right foot past your left so that you achieve a right forward stance and execute a right spear hand strike.

(22 & 23) Make a three-quarter counterclockwise turn so that you achieve a left back stance, and execute a left knife hand strike. (24) Step your right foot past your left, but 45 degrees to the right of your left foot, and execute a right knife hand strike from the right back stance.

(25) Move your right foot 135 degrees clockwise so that you achieve a right back stance and execute a right knife hand strike. (26) Step your left foot past your right at a 45-degree angle to the left so that you achieve a left back stance and execute a left knife hand strike. (27) Move your left foot 45

degrees counterclockwise so that you achieve a left forward stance and execute a right outside block. (28) From the same stance, execute a right punch while you simultaneously make a right front kick.

(29) Drop your kicking foot to the floor so that you achieve a right forward stance and execute a left reverse punch. (30) From the same stance, execute a left outside block. (31) Simultaneously execute a left punch and a left front kick. (32) Drop your kicking foot to the floor so that you achieve a left forward stance and execute a right reverse punch. (33 & 34) Step your right foot past your left so that you achieve a right forward stance and execute a right outside block.

31

32

31 Side View

32 Side View

33

34

(35 & 36) Pivoting on your right foot, make a three-quarter turn so that you achieve a left forward stance and simultaneously execute a left low block. (37 & 38) From the same stance, cock your left fist over your right shoulder and execute a left outside knife hand block. (39) Step through with your right foot, 45 degrees to the right and execute a right high block. (40) Move your right foot 135 degrees clockwise so that you achieve a right forward stance and execute a right low block. (41 & 42) From the same stance, execute a high right knife hand block. (43) Step your left foot ahead and 45 degrees to the right, so that you achieve a left forward stance and simultaneously execute a left high block. (44) Move your left foot back into your right and assume the ready position to close the form.

FIGHTING FORMS DRILLS

The fighting form differs from the classical forms since it is more realistic. Although it contains the grace, rhythm and power of the classical form, it brings the speed of its moves up to a fighting realism. The classical form, on the other hand, more closely resembles a dance.

Fighting forms can be used as "aggression builders" when performed as though you are really fighting, with full speed and full power. The technique portions of these forms, however, must not be sacrificed to speed, or you will be defeating their purpose. When done properly, they will render endurance, rhythm and speed. This means that you must master the fighting form in the four phase method of slow motion, half-speed, full-speed and red-line.

(KICK FORM)

(1) Begin by assuming the left forward stance with your fists at medium height. (2) Slide your right foot forward into your left foot. (3 & 4) Execute a high left front kick.

(5) Drop your kicking foot to the floor and begin to turn your upper torso clockwise. (6) Complete the 180-degree clockwise turn so that you achieve a right forward stance. (7) Slide your left foot forward into your right foot. (8 & 9) Execute a right high front kick. (10) Drop your kicking foot to the floor and (11) turn your upper torso 180 degrees counterclockwise so that you achieve a left forward stance. (12 & 13) Execute a high left front kick.

13

(14) Drop your kicking foot down toward the floor. (15 & 16) As your kicking foot touches the floor, immediately execute a right front kick. (17) Return your kicking foot to the floor behind your left foot so that you achieve a left forward stance. (18 & 19) Execute another right front kick as soon as your right foot hits the floor. (20) Drop your kicking foot straight down to the floor so that you momentarily achieve a right fighting stance. (21) Turn your upper torso 180 degrees counterclockwise so that you are now in left fighting stance.

16

19

(22) Slide your right foot forward into your left foot. (23 & 24) As your right foot touches your left, immediately execute a left round-house kick. (25) Drop your kicking foot straight down to the floor from the point of impact. (26) As your left foot hits the floor, turn your upper torso 180 degrees clockwise so that you achieve a left back stance. (27) Slide your left foot forward into your right foot. (28 & 29) Execute a right roundhouse kick. (30) Begin turning your upper torso counterclockwise as you drop your kicking foot straight down toward the floor.

31

(31) When your kicking foot reaches the floor, you should be finished with the 180-degree counterclockwise turn of your upper torso, and you should be in a left back stance. (32 & 33) Execute a right spinning roundhouse kick. (34—36) Drop your kicking leg straight down to the floor and turn your upper torso 180 degrees counterclockwise so that you achieve a left back stance. (37) Slide your right foot forward into your left foot. (38) Execute a high left side kick. (39) Drop your kicking foot straight down to the floor and begin to turn your upper torso clockwise.

34

37

(40) When your kicking foot reaches the floor, you should be finished with the 180-degree clockwise turn of your upper torso, and you should be in a right back stance. (41) Slide your left foot forward into your right foot. (42 & 43) Execute a high right side kick. (44) Drop your kicking foot straight down to the floor and begin to turn your upper torso counterclockwise. (45) When your kicking foot reaches the floor, you should be finished with the 180-degree counterclockwise turn of your upper torso, and you should be in a left back stance. (46 & 47) Execute a right spinning side kick. (48) Drop your kicking foot straight down to the floor and turn your torso 180 degrees counterclockwise so that you achieve a left back stance.

(49) Slide your right foot forward, behind and slightly beyond your left foot. (50 & 51) Execute a high left back kick. (52) Drop your kicking foot straight down to the floor and begin turning your upper torso clockwise. (53) When your kicking foot reaches the floor, you should be finished with the 180-degree clockwise turn of your upper torso, and you should begin immediately to slide that foot toward your right foot. (54) Complete the slide of your left foot when it is slightly beyond your right foot. (55) Execute a high right back kick. (56) Drop your kicking foot straight down to the floor so that you are in a left fighting stance. (57) Lift your right foot and, pivoting on your left foot, begin turning your body clockwise.

58

59

(58) Follow through with the turn
and execute a right spinning back
kick. (59) Drop your kicking foot
straight down to the floor so that
you achieve a right fighting stance
to end the form.

(SPEED BLITZ FORMS)

The *speed blitz* drills combine all of the desirable elements which make for helpful practice. They sharpen your technique, while concentrating on raising your level of speed, power and ultimately your endurance. They are much shorter forms, and therefore are easier to memorize. After you have perfected their moves by practicing in slow motion, half-speed, and full-speed, strive for their greatest effect by performing them at red-line. You will find that they can vastly increase your stamina.

SPEED BLITZ (A)

(1) Begin by assuming a left fighting stance with your fists at medium height.
(2) Lunge forward off your rear foot while you simultaneously execute a left high block.
(3) From the same stance, execute a right reverse punch

while retracting your other fist to your hip. (4) Maintaining your right reverse punch posture, execute a high right front kick. (5) Return your right foot to the floor so that you remain in a left forward fighting stance.

SPEED BLITZ (B)

(1) Begin by assuming a right forward stance with your fists at medium height. (2 & 3) From this stance, execute a right side kick and a right back knuckle strike simultaneously. (4 & 5) As your kicking foot is dropped straight down to the

floor, cock your right fist across your chest and execute another right back knuckle strike. (6) Turn your hips counterclockwise and execute a left reverse punch while retracting your right fist to your hip.

SPEED BLITZ (C)

(1) Begin by assuming a left forward fighting stance with your fists at medium height. (2) Slide your left foot back toward your right while you execute a high right reverse punch. (3 & 4) Maintaining your right reverse punch, execute a high right front kick. (5 & 6) As kicking foot drops straight down to the floor, execute a left reverse punch. (7 & 8) From this position, execute a high left crescent kick. (9 & 10) Follow through with the kick and when your kicking foot reaches the floor in a left forward stance, execute a right reverse punch.

SPEED BLITZ (D)

(1) Begin by assuming a left forward fighting stance with your fists at medium height. (2 & 3) Lunge forward off your rear foot and simultaneously execute a left back knuckle strike. (4 & 5) Pivot your body around clockwise on your forward foot (the left, in this case). (6 & 7) Making use of your clockwise momentum, execute a right spinning back kick. (8 & 9) Follow through with the momentum of the kick so that you are in a right fighting stance when your kicking foot touches the floor, and immediately execute a right back knuckle strike. (10) Continue turning your hips clockwise and execute a left reverse punch while you retract your right fist to your hip.

ONE-STEP SPARRING TECHNIQUES

Although the one-steps offered on the following pages may appear artificial in the context of a fighting situation, their primary purpose is to build different parts of you into a fighting machine. In the long run, they will give you far more control over your opponent. For this reason, they should be practiced at full power and full speed after you have mastered their many techniques.

Only two sparring exercises are offered in this volume, in hopes that you will be able to create your own exercises after having mastered them. Remember that technique is just as important as speed and power.

ONE-STEP SPARRING TECHNIQUE No. 1

(1) Begin by facing your opponent in a right forward fighting stance with your fists held at medium height. (2) As your opponent steps through and attempts a right punch at your head, quickly move your right foot forward and 45 degrees to the right. Execute a left hand knife hand block, and (3) counter with a right knife hand strike to his neck. (4) Immediately execute a left reverse punch to his midsection from the same stance.

(5 & 6) Execute a right cross elbow strike to your opponent's jaw, being sure to follow through with the blow. (7) Execute a right bottom fist strike to your opponent's face by reversing the direction of your previous blow. (8) Completely follow through with your bottom fist and smoothly execute a left reverse punch to the midsection.

(9 & 10) Turn your hips in the opposite direction as you execute a right uppercut punch and follow through completely. (11) Reverse the direction of your punch and execute a right downward elbow strike to the throat or upper chest. (12) Recover to a left forward fighting stance by stepping back with your right leg.

ONE-STEP SPARRING TECHNIQUE No. 2

(1) Begin by facing your opponent in a left forward fighting stance with your fists at medium height. (2 & 3) As your opponent steps through and attempts a right punch at your head, move your left leg to the left, executing a right knife hand block. (4) Grasp your opponent's punching hand at the wrist with your blocking hand, turn your hips clockwise, and execute a left reverse punch to his ribs.

(5) Grasp your opponent's right wrist with both of your hands while you step your left leg across and in back of your right so that you are facing away from your opponent. (6) Snap your opponent's arm down on your left shoulder with an elbow break technique, while freeing your left hand for a strike. (7) Execute a left reverse elbow strike to your opponent's ribs while you maintain hold of his wrist with your right hand. (8—10) Execute a wrist throw by pulling your opponent's wrist downward behind him while stepping your left foot around your right 180 degrees counterclockwise. Pull downward until your opponent loses balance and falls to the floor. (11) Recover to the left forward stance to end the technique.

BLACK BELT™ *VIDEO PRESENTS*